# Abiding in Christ's Presence

## A Forty Day Spiritual Journey

Richard Blackaby and Bob Royall

© 2023 Blackaby Ministries International

No part of this book may be reproduced or transmitted in any form or by any means, electronic or mechanical, including photocopying and recording, or by any information storage or retrieval system, except as may be expressly permitted in writing by the publisher. Requests for permission should be addressed in writing to BMI; P.O. Box 1035 Jonesboro, GA 30237.

ISBN 978-1-7350872-8-3

Subject heading: Abiding in Christ's Presence

Unless indicated otherwise, Scripture quotations are taken from the Holy Bible, NEW INTERNATIONAL VERSION®. Copyright © 1973, 1978, 1984 by Biblica Inc. All rights reserved worldwide. Used by permission. Scripture quotations marked NKJV are taken from the New King James Version. Copyright © 1979, 1980, 1982, Thomas Nelson Inc., Publishers. Scripture quotations from the ESV® Bible (The Holy Bible, English Standard Version®), Copyright © 2001 by Crossway, a publishing ministry of Good News Publishers. Used by permission. All rights reserved.

To order additional copies of this resource, write to BMI; P.O. Box 1035 Jonesboro, GA 30237; email resources@blackaby.org; fax 770-603-2900; phone toll free 877-311-2626; or order online at blackabystore.org.

Printed in the United States of America

Blackaby Ministries International; P.O. Box 1035 Jonesboro, GA 30237

# Table of Contents

| | |
|---|---|
| Preface | 5 |
| Introduction and Overview | 7 |
| Using the Seven Realities as a Guide for Spiritual Reflection | 9 |
| Suggestions for Using this Spiritual Journal in Groups and with Partners | 13 |
| Daily Spiritual Journal | 15 |
| End-of-Journal Reflection | 57 |
| Prayer Requests/Answered Prayers | 60 |
| Ways I/We Have Seen God Working | 62 |
| What I Have Learned about God's Character, Purposes, Ways | 63 |
| Reasons for Gratitude | 64 |
| Additional BMI Resources | 65 |
| About the Authors | 67 |

# Preface

The psalms were written for ordinary people facing life's challenges. They begin with the observation, "Blessed is the man who walks not in the counsel of the wicked, nor stands in the way of sinners, nor sits in the seat of scoffers; but his delight is in the law of the Lord, and on his law he meditates day and night. He is like a tree planted by streams of water that yields its fruit in its season, and its leaf does not wither. In all that he does, he prospers." (Psalm 1:1-3). This is the key to successful living.

The world views life's events one way, while God sees them entirely differently. God's ways are not ours (Isaiah 55:8-9). The only way to see your life from God's perspective is to regularly spend time with him, reflecting upon his word. God is always at work around you. However, if you are disoriented to God and his ways, you will fail to recognize when he is working out his purposes in your life.

The wise person begins each day in God's presence. Let God's Word fill your heart and mind. Allow the Holy Spirit to alert you to what he knows you will face that day. Let him adjust your plans so you are on God's agenda. Let the Holy Spirit pinpoint areas in your life that are displeasing to him. Welcome his pruning when he removes from your life anything that is hindering your fruitfulness. Ask God to elevate your thinking and viewpoints until his thoughts become your thoughts.

The world is opposed to godly thinking and values. It insists that you conform your viewpoints to match those of secular society. Only by regularly meditating on God's Word can you free yourself from the world's gravitational pull and set your mind on things above. We pray that this journal helps you to hear from God. If you turn your attention to God each day, you may be surprised at how often you notice God at work around you.

## The value of spiritual journaling

Psalm 106:6-13 (ESV) reminds believers of the importance of "remembering" what God has done for us (underlining has been added for emphasis):

> *Both we and our fathers have sinned; we have committed iniquity; we have done wickedness.*
>
> *Our fathers, when they were in Egypt, <u>did not consider your wondrous works; they did not remember the abundance of your steadfast love</u>, but rebelled by the sea, at the Red Sea.*
>
> *Yet he saved them for his name's sake, that he might make known his mighty power. He rebuked the Red Sea, and it became dry, and he led them through the deep as through a desert. So he saved them from the hand of the foe and redeemed them from the power of the enemy. And the waters covered their adversaries; not one of them was left. Then they believed his words; they sang his praise.*
>
> *<u>But they soon forgot his works; they did not wait for his counsel</u>.*

The Bible is replete with admonitions to reflect carefully on God's character, his purposes, and his ways. Take time to be alone with God, daily, read his Word, and reflect on his character. Dedicate yourself to prayer and recognizing his activity around you. By doing so, you will build a spiritual legacy that will last for generations!

# Introduction and Overview

## Purpose

This journal is designed to help you know God better and to deepen your relationship with him. As you spend time reading the Bible and praying, your spiritual eyes will be opened to ways God is at work around you and to what he is saying to you. When you respond in faith to him, obeying his promptings, he will strengthen you as a spiritual leader.

## Elements

The elements of this journal include the following:

### Today I am grateful for...

Psalm 100:4-5 urges God's people to "Enter his gates with thanksgiving, and his courts with praise! Give thanks to him; bless his name! For the LORD is good; his steadfast love endures forever, and his faithfulness to all generations." When we begin a spiritual habit of giving thanks to the Lord for who he is and for specific ways he has blessed us, we experience a deepening fellowship with him.

### Bible reading

You may follow whatever Bible-reading plan you choose. If you are unsure where to begin, here are some good options: Exodus, Gospel of John, Philippians, Gospel of Luke, or Romans. Rather than lightly reading over large swaths of the Bible, we encourage you to read less, but reflect more deeply, perhaps a chapter or two per day.

### Insight verse

Ask God to draw your heart to a specific verse or two. Write it out in the designated section and then reflect on what the verse reveals about God's nature or character, his purposes, and/or how he works.

### Adjustments/prayer response

Record a prayer response to God based on your chosen verse. For example, for a verse that says, "God is love," you might write, "Thank you, O God, for loving me even when I am unlovable! I welcome and receive your love!"

### To do

List your Priorities for today and surrender them to God.

### A thought for your day

Each day's journal includes a brief thought from Richard Blackaby to focus your attention on God and his ways.

### Reflect back

Ask God to reveal his work around you as you reflect on your day. Jot down your spiritual insights, such as an answered prayer or an experience of God's provision. Complete this step either today or tomorrow morning prior to your Bible reading.

Take a moment to reflect on the emotions you felt during the events of the past day. They may provide insights as to the state of your relationship with God.

# Using the Seven Realities as a Guide for Spiritual Reflection

The Seven Realities[1] provide important reference points for spiritual reflection. As you reflect back on each day, ask God to show you how he has worked around, within, and through you and others. Here are the Realities:

## 1. God is always at work around you.

God is always at work, accomplishing his eternal purposes. He is not limited to certain types of government, economies, or political freedoms. God's kingdom is continually expanding, person by person, around the world. God is always at work around you, your family, church, neighborhood, and workplace, whether you recognize what he is doing or not. If you remain spiritually alert, you will recognize God's activity around your life. Watch for things only God can do, like convicting people of their sin or drawing people closer to God.

## 2. God pursues a continuing love relationship with you that is real and personal.

God's greatest desire for you is that you would love him with all your heart, mind, soul, and strength. He does not merely want you to believe in him or obey him; he wants you to enter into a dynamic, growing, loving relationship with your Creator, Savior, and Lord. Be alert throughout the day to the numerous ways God expresses his love to you and draws you into a closer walk with him.

---

[1]. *Experiencing God: Knowing and Doing the Will of God* by Henry T. Blackaby, Richard Blackaby, Mike Blackaby, Claude V. King, Nashville: Broadman and Holman, 2022.

## 3. God invites you to join him in his work.

It is breathtaking to consider that almighty God, ruler of the universe, delights in involving us, his creatures, in his eternal purposes. When God reveals to you what he is doing in someone's life or in your church, that is his invitation for you to join him in his work. Rather than trying to initiate new activities for God, respond immediately to the invitations God extends to you throughout your day.

## 4. God speaks by the Holy Spirit through the Bible, prayer, circumstances, and the church (other believers) to reveal himself, his purposes, and his ways.

The Bible testifies that God speaks to his people. Speaking audibly is only one of countless ways God communicates. God's Holy Spirit resides within every believer. The Spirit knows the will of the Father, and he will reveal it to you, if you pay attention. The Spirit will speak in four primary ways. First and foremost, he will speak through the Bible. The Spirit will take Scripture and apply it specifically to your life. God will never speak anything contrary to what he has clearly revealed in the Bible. Second, the Spirit will guide you as you pray, for prayer is a two-way conversation. Take time to listen, remaining attentive to God and to any inner promptings you may sense from him as you pray. Third, God will speak through the circumstances in your life. Open and closed doors might be one way he speaks. Finally, the Spirit will speak through other people into your life. This is why it is imperative for you to be immersing yourself regularly in

God's Word and prayer, asking the Holy Spirit to interpret your circumstances and surrounding yourself with godly friends who can be God's mouthpiece into your life.

## 5. God's invitation to join him in his work always leads to a crisis of belief that requires faith and action.

God does God-sized, eternal work. At times, the scale and significance of our assigments can overwhelm us or make us feel inadequate. We can face a crisis of belief in which we question whether what God intends to do in and through us is possible. In those moments, we must believe God will equip, empower, and provide for whatever he calls us to do. Pay attention to the moments when you experience fear, reluctance, or lack of faith, especially when you sense God is calling you to something you cannot accomplish without his help. Reflect in your journal and record what you experienced, how you felt, and how you responded to God's invitation. What does God want you to learn from this encounter?

## 6. You must make major adjustments to join God in his work.

You cannot stay where you are and go with God! Obedience to God will inevitably require you to make changes in your life. These adjustments may involve your attitudes, money, time, commitments, and your job. Be fully prepared to make whatever changes are necessary so you are in position to obey fully and join him in his work.

## 7. You come to know God by experience as you join him and he accomplishes his work through you.

God does not merely want you to believe in him; he wants you to experience him. As God leads you into his activity and equips and provides everything you need, you will experience the very things you have read about in the Bible. Spiritual journaling provides an opportunity to remember and reflect on the many ways God has been working in and around your life.

# Suggestions for Using this Spiritual Journal in Groups and with Partners

One of the enduring values small groups offer is the privilege of sharing our spiritual lives together. Acts 2:42-47 reveals the power that spiritual community had for the Early Church.

> And they continued steadfastly in the apostles' doctrine and fellowship, in the breaking of bread, and in prayers. Then fear came upon every soul, and many wonders and signs were done through the apostles. Now all who believed were together, and had all things in common, and sold their possessions and goods, and divided them among all, as anyone had need. So continuing daily with one accord in the temple, and breaking bread from house to house, they ate their food with gladness and simplicity of heart, praising God and having favor with all the people. And the Lord added to the church daily those who were being saved. (NKJV)

The early believers shared everything, structured their lives around the apostles' teaching and Scripture, prayed together, and testified to the ways God was actively working in their midst.

This Spiritual Journal provides a structure for intentional reflection on:

- Gratitude
- Scripture
- Prayer
- Activity of God

These elements provide an ideal basis for spiritual fellowship within small groups. Whether the journal is used on its own, or in conjunction with study of a particular book of the Bible, or discipleship study such as *Experiencing God*, participants can share the personal insights from the week prior.

Here are some prompt questions that may stimulate discussions:

- What one reason for gratitude you recorded in your journal that stands out most from your week? Explain why.
- Read one day's focal verse from the week that meant the most to you. What did you learn about God's character, purposes, and/or ways? What adjustments/prayer response did you record for this verse?
- Have you experienced an answered prayer? If so, share it with the group. What did God teach you through it?
- How have you noticed God at work around you this week? How did you respond?
- If you have a prayer request, share it with the group.
- Is there an issue, faith challenge, or opportunity about you which require the group's help with spiritual discernment? If so, share your question or concern with group members, allowing them to pray for you and ask clarifying questions to help you gain insight regarding what God is doing.

At the end of the journal, the group may spend focused time sharing insights they gained through the End-of-Journal Reflections. Always allow ample time for prayer and giving thanks to God.

# Daily Spiritual Journal

Daily Spiritual Journal

## Day 1

Date:
Passage:

**Today, I am grateful for...**

**Insight verse(s) (write out focus verse for deeper reflection)**

**What this passage reveals about God's character, his purposes, or his ways**

**Adjustments/prayer response: (my response to God's word)**

**Priorities for today**
- 
- 
- 

---

**A thought for your day...**
You cannot stay where you are and go with God.

---

**Reflect back**
What do you sense God has been doing around you, your family, your work, your world? How have you responded?

Daily Spiritual Journal

| **Day 2** | Date:<br>Passage: |

**Today, I am grateful for...**

**Insight verse(s) (write out focus verse for deeper reflection)**

**What this passage reveals about God's character, his purposes, or his ways**

**Adjustments/prayer response: (my response to God's word)**

**Priorities for today**
- 
- 
- 

### A thought for your day...
You can't give to others what you don't have yourself.

**Reflect back**
What do you sense God has been doing around you, your family, your work, your world? How have you responded?

Daily Spiritual Journal

## Day 3

Date:
Passage:

**Today, I am grateful for...**

**Insight verse(s) (write out focus verse for deeper reflection)**

**What this passage reveals about God's character, his purposes, or his ways**

**Adjustments/prayer response: (my response to God's word)**

**Priorities for today**

- 
- 
- 

### A thought for your day...
Before Christ sends you out, he draws you in.

**Reflect back**
What do you sense God has been doing around you, your family, your work, your world? How have you responded?

Daily Spiritual Journal

## Day 4

Date:
Passage:

**Today, I am grateful for...**

**Insight verse(s) (write out focus verse for deeper reflection)**

**What this passage reveals about God's character, his purposes, or his ways**

**Adjustments/prayer response: (my response to God's word)**

**Priorities for today**

- ☐
- ☐
- ☐

### A thought for your day...
You cannot follow a crucified Christ
unless you take up your cross.

**Reflect back**
What do you sense God has been doing around you, your family, your work, your world? How have you responded?

Daily Spiritual Journal

## Day 5

Date:
Passage:

**Today, I am grateful for...**

**Insight verse(s) (write out focus verse for deeper reflection)**

**What this passage reveals about God's character, his purposes, or his ways**

**Adjustments/prayer response: (my response to God's word)**

**Priorities for today**
- 
- 
- 

### A thought for your day...
Mountaintops are not designed to be permanent,
but preparatory.

**Reflect back**
What do you sense God has been doing around you, your family, your work, your world? How have you responded?

## Day 6

Date:
Passage:

**Today, I am grateful for...**

---
---

**Insight verse(s) (write out focus verse for deeper reflection)**

---
---

**What this passage reveals about God's character, his purposes, or his ways**

---
---

**Adjustments/prayer response: (my response to God's word)**

---
---

**Priorities for today**

- ☐ _____
- ☐ _____
- ☐ _____

### A thought for your day...
Never forget; people are not the enemy.

**Reflect back**
What do you sense God has been doing around you, your family, your work, your world? How have you responded?

---
---
---

Daily Spiritual Journal

## Day 7

Date:
Passage:

**Today, I am grateful for...**

**Insight verse(s) (write out focus verse for deeper reflection)**

**What this passage reveals about God's character, his purposes, or his ways**

**Adjustments/prayer response: (my response to God's word)**

**Priorities for today**

- 
- 
- 

> **A thought for your day...**
> It may not be that God is not speaking,
> but that you are not hearing.

**Reflect back**
What do you sense God has been doing around you, your family, your work, your world? How have you responded?

Daily Spiritual Journal

## Day 8

Date:
Passage:

**Today, I am grateful for...**

**Insight verse(s) (write out focus verse for deeper reflection)**

**What this passage reveals about God's character, his purposes, or his ways**

**Adjustments/prayer response: (my response to God's word)**

**Priorities for today**

- 
- 
- 

### A thought for your day...
Spiritual leaders take people from where they are to where God wants them to be.

**Reflect back**
What do you sense God has been doing around you, your family, your work, your world? How have you responded?

Daily Spiritual Journal

## Day 9

Date:
Passage:

**Today, I am grateful for...**

**Insight verse(s) (write out focus verse for deeper reflection)**

**What this passage reveals about God's character, his purposes, or his ways**

**Adjustments/prayer response: (my response to God's word)**

**Priorities for today**
- 
- 
- 

> **A thought for your day...**
> If people are not following,
> seek God's perspective on your leadership.

**Reflect back**
What do you sense God has been doing around you, your family, your work, your world? How have you responded?

Daily Spiritual Journal

**Day 10**  Date:
       Passage:

**Today, I am grateful for...**

**Insight verse(s) (write out focus verse for deeper reflection)**

**What this passage reveals about God's character, his purposes, or his ways**

**Adjustments/prayer response: (my response to God's word)**

**Priorities for today**
- 
- 
- 

**A thought for your day...**
One of the best ways to bless those you lead is
for you to keep growing.

**Reflect back**
What do you sense God has been doing around you, your family, your work, your world? How have you responded?

Daily Spiritual Journal

## Day 11

Date:
Passage:

**Today, I am grateful for...**

**Insight verse(s) (write out focus verse for deeper reflection)**

**What this passage reveals about God's character, his purposes, or his ways**

**Adjustments/prayer response: (my response to God's word)**

**Priorities for today**
- 
- 
- 

---

**A thought for your day...**
Be careful! Giving people your best
may inadvertently rob them of God's best.

---

**Reflect back**
What do you sense God has been doing around you, your family, your work, your world? How have you responded?

## Day 12

Date:
Passage:

**Today, I am grateful for...**

_____
_____

**Insight verse(s) (write out focus verse for deeper reflection)**

_____
_____

**What this passage reveals about God's character, his purposes, or his ways**

_____
_____

**Adjustments/prayer response: (my response to God's word)**

_____
_____

**Priorities for today**

- _____
- _____
- _____

### A thought for your day...
When God invites you to join him in his work,
what you do next reveals what you believe about him.

**Reflect back**
What do you sense God has been doing around you, your family, your work, your world? How have you responded?

_____
_____

Daily Spiritual Journal

## Day 13

Date:
Passage:

**Today, I am grateful for...**

**Insight verse(s) (write out focus verse for deeper reflection)**

**What this passage reveals about God's character, his purposes, or his ways**

**Adjustments/prayer response: (my response to God's word)**

**Priorities for today**
- 
- 
- 

**A thought for your day...**
Great leaders don't make excuses, they make things better.

**Reflect back**
What do you sense God has been doing around you, your family, your work, your world? How have you responded?

Daily Spiritual Journal

## Day 14

Date:
Passage:

**Today, I am grateful for...**

**Insight verse(s) (write out focus verse for deeper reflection)**

**What this passage reveals about God's character, his purposes, or his ways**

**Adjustments/prayer response: (my response to God's word)**

**Priorities for today**

- 
- 
- 

### A thought for your day...
Are you raising up followers, or leaders?

**Reflect back**
What do you sense God has been doing around you, your family, your work, your world? How have you responded?

Daily Spiritual Journal

### Day 15

Date:
Passage:

**Today, I am grateful for...**

**Insight verse(s) (write out focus verse for deeper reflection)**

**What this passage reveals about God's character, his purposes, or his ways**

**Adjustments/prayer response: (my response to God's word)**

**Priorities for today**
- 
- 
- 

**A thought for your day...**
How is your leadership a blessing to those you lead?

**Reflect back**
What do you sense God has been doing around you, your family, your work, your world? How have you responded?

Daily Spiritual Journal

## Day 16

Date:
Passage:

**Today, I am grateful for...**

**Insight verse(s) (write out focus verse for deeper reflection)**

**What this passage reveals about God's character, his purposes, or his ways**

**Adjustments/prayer response: (my response to God's word)**

**Priorities for today**

- 
- 
- 

**A thought for your day...**
God is always at work around you.
Are you noticing what he is doing?

**Reflect back**
What do you sense God has been doing around you, your family, your work, your world? How have you responded?

Daily Spiritual Journal

## Day 17

Date:
Passage:

**Today, I am grateful for...**

**Insight verse(s) (write out focus verse for deeper reflection)**

**What this passage reveals about God's character, his purposes, or his ways**

**Adjustments/prayer response: (my response to God's word)**

**Priorities for today**

- 
- 
- 

### A thought for your day...
Rich treasures can be uncovered from reflecting on our failures as well as our successes.

**Reflect back**
What do you sense God has been doing around you, your family, your work, your world? How have you responded?

## Day 18

Date:
Passage:

**Today, I am grateful for...**

_____

_____

**Insight verse(s) (write out focus verse for deeper reflection)**

_____

_____

**What this passage reveals about God's character, his purposes, or his ways**

_____

_____

**Adjustments/prayer response: (my response to God's word)**

_____

_____

**Priorities for today**

- ▪ _____
- ▪ _____
- ▪ _____

---

**A thought for your day...**
God is far more concerned with
who you are than what you are doing.

---

**Reflect back**
What do you sense God has been doing around you, your family, your work, your world? How have you responded?

_____

_____

Daily Spiritual Journal

## Day 19

Date:
Passage:

**Today, I am grateful for...**

**Insight verse(s) (write out focus verse for deeper reflection)**

**What this passage reveals about God's character, his purposes, or his ways**

**Adjustments/prayer response: (my response to God's word)**

**Priorities for today**
- 
- 
- 

### A thought for your day...
The fruit of your life flows out of the intimacy
and vibrancy of your walk with God

**Reflect back**
What do you sense God has been doing around you, your family, your work, your world? How have you responded?

Daily Spiritual Journal

| Day 20 | Date:
Passage: |

Today, I am grateful for...

Insight verse(s) (write out focus verse for deeper reflection)

What this passage reveals about God's character, his purposes, or his ways

Adjustments/prayer response: (my response to God's word)

Priorities for today

- 
- 
- 

### A thought for your day...
Your life brings glory to God when
you produce much fruit (John 15:8)

**Reflect back**
What do you sense God has been doing around you, your family, your work, your world? How have you responded?

Daily Spiritual Journal

## Day 21

Date:
Passage:

**Today, I am grateful for...**

**Insight verse(s) (write out focus verse for deeper reflection)**

**What this passage reveals about God's character, his purposes, or his ways**

**Adjustments/prayer response: (my response to God's word)**

**Priorities for today**

- 
- 
- 

### A thought for your day...
The unmistakable evidence you are abiding in Christ is that your life overflows with the joy of the Lord (John 15:11)

**Reflect back**
What do you sense God has been doing around you, your family, your work, your world? How have you responded?

## Day 22

Date:
Passage:

**Today, I am grateful for...**

**Insight verse(s) (write out focus verse for deeper reflection)**

**What this passage reveals about God's character, his purposes, or his ways**

**Adjustments/prayer response: (my response to God's word)**

**Priorities for today**

- 
- 
- 

### A thought for your day...
God's ways are not your ways! (Is. 55:8-9). If your plan makes perfect sense to you, it probably did not come from God!

**Reflect back**
What do you sense God has been doing around you, your family, your work, your world? How have you responded?

Daily Spiritual Journal

## Day 23

Date:
Passage:

**Today, I am grateful for...**

**Insight verse(s) (write out focus verse for deeper reflection)**

**What this passage reveals about God's character, his purposes, or his ways**

**Adjustments/prayer response: (my response to God's word)**

**Priorities for today**
- 
- 
- 

### A thought for your day...
If you know what God wants you to do
and yet you have not done it, you are sinning (James 4:17)

**Reflect back**
What do you sense God has been doing around you, your family, your work, your world? How have you responded?

Daily Spiritual Journal

## Day 24

Date:
Passage:

**Today, I am grateful for...**

**Insight verse(s) (write out focus verse for deeper reflection)**

**What this passage reveals about God's character, his purposes, or his ways**

**Adjustments/prayer response: (my response to God's word)**

**Priorities for today**

- 
- 
- 

### A thought for your day...
Without faith, it is impossible to please God (Heb. 11:6).
Where in your life are you currently living by faith?

**Reflect back**
What do you sense God has been doing around you, your family, your work, your world? How have you responded?

Daily Spiritual Journal

## Day 25

Date:
Passage:

**Today, I am grateful for...**

**Insight verse(s) (write out focus verse for deeper reflection)**

**What this passage reveals about God's character, his purposes, or his ways**

**Adjustments/prayer response: (my response to God's word)**

**Priorities for today**

- 
- 
- 

### A thought for your day...
God is certainly your friend, but are you his friend? (John 15:14)

**Reflect back**
What do you sense God has been doing around you, your family, your work, your world? How have you responded?

Daily Spiritual Journal

## Day 26

Date:
Passage:

**Today, I am grateful for...**

**Insight verse(s) (write out focus verse for deeper reflection)**

**What this passage reveals about God's character, his purposes, or his ways**

**Adjustments/prayer response: (my response to God's word)**

**Priorities for today**

- 
- 
- 

### A thought for your day...
God has given you every resource necessary to resist temptation, if you want to (1 Cor. 10:13)

**Reflect back**
What do you sense God has been doing around you, your family, your work, your world? How have you responded?

## Day 27

Date:
Passage:

**Today, I am grateful for...**

**Insight verse(s) (write out focus verse for deeper reflection)**

**What this passage reveals about God's character, his purposes, or his ways**

**Adjustments/prayer response: (my response to God's word)**

**Priorities for today**

- 
- 
- 

### A thought for your day...
Why hold on to your worries when God invites you to cast them on him? (1 Peter 5:7)

**Reflect back**
What do you sense God has been doing around you, your family, your work, your world? How have you responded?

Daily Spiritual Journal

| **Day 28** | Date:<br>Passage: |

**Today, I am grateful for...**

**Insight verse(s) (write out focus verse for deeper reflection)**

**What this passage reveals about God's character, his purposes, or his ways**

**Adjustments/prayer response: (my response to God's word)**

**Priorities for today**
- 
- 
- 

**A thought for your day...**
Do your words build people up or tear them down?
(Ephesians 4:29)

**Reflect back**
What do you sense God has been doing around you, your family, your work, your world? How have you responded?

Daily Spiritual Journal

## Day 29

Date:
Passage:

**Today, I am grateful for...**

**Insight verse(s) (write out focus verse for deeper reflection)**

**What this passage reveals about God's character, his purposes, or his ways**

**Adjustments/prayer response: (my response to God's word)**

**Priorities for today**

- 
- 
- 

### A thought for your day...
There is absolutely no evil, no power, no enemy, and no circumstance that can separate you from God's amazing love for you (Romans 8:35-39)

**Reflect back**
What do you sense God has been doing around you, your family, your work, your world? How have you responded?

Daily Spiritual Journal

## Day 30

Date:
Passage:

**Today, I am grateful for...**

**Insight verse(s) (write out focus verse for deeper reflection)**

**What this passage reveals about God's character, his purposes, or his ways**

**Adjustments/prayer response: (my response to God's word)**

**Priorities for today**
- 
- 
- 

### A thought for your day...
Call to God and he will reveal truths you do not know (Jer. 33:3)

**Reflect back**
What do you sense God has been doing around you, your family, your work, your world? How have you responded?

Daily Spiritual Journal

## Day 31

Date:
Passage:

**Today, I am grateful for...**

**Insight verse(s) (write out focus verse for deeper reflection)**

**What this passage reveals about God's character, his purposes, or his ways**

**Adjustments/prayer response: (my response to God's word)**

**Priorities for today**

- 
- 
- 

### A thought for your day...
What God purposes, he is wholly committed to bring to pass
(Isaiah 46:11)

**Reflect back**
What do you sense God has been doing around you, your family, your work, your world? How have you responded?

Daily Spiritual Journal

## Day 32

Date:
Passage:

**Today, I am grateful for...**

**Insight verse(s) (write out focus verse for deeper reflection)**

**What this passage reveals about God's character, his purposes, or his ways**

**Adjustments/prayer response: (my response to God's word)**

**Priorities for today**
- 
- 
- 

### A thought for your day...
Delight yourself in the Lord, and everything else you need will be given to you (Psalm 37:4)

**Reflect back**
What do you sense God has been doing around you, your family, your work, your world? How have you responded?

Daily Spiritual Journal

## Day 33

Date:
Passage:

**Today, I am grateful for...**

**Insight verse(s) (write out focus verse for deeper reflection)**

**What this passage reveals about God's character, his purposes, or his ways**

**Adjustments/prayer response: (my response to God's word)**

**Priorities for today**
- 
- 
- 

### A thought for your day...
What is the one thing you must do? (Phil. 3:13)

**Reflect back**
What do you sense God has been doing around you, your family, your work, your world? How have you responded?

## Day 34

Date:
Passage:

**Today, I am grateful for...**

**Insight verse(s) (write out focus verse for deeper reflection)**

**What this passage reveals about God's character, his purposes, or his ways**

**Adjustments/prayer response: (my response to God's word)**

**Priorities for today**

- 
- 
- 

### A thought for your day...
Are you hesitating to take up your cross? (Matt. 16:24). There is no such thing as cross-less Christianity.

**Reflect back**
What do you sense God has been doing around you, your family, your work, your world? How have you responded?

Daily Spiritual Journal

**Day 35**  Date:
         Passage:

**Today, I am grateful for...**

**Insight verse(s) (write out focus verse for deeper reflection)**

**What this passage reveals about God's character, his purposes, or his ways**

**Adjustments/prayer response: (my response to God's word)**

**Priorities for today**
- 
- 
- 

**A thought for your day...**
God is your fortress (Psalm 31). You can find refuge in him.

**Reflect back**
What do you sense God has been doing around you, your family, your work, your world? How have you responded?

Daily Spiritual Journal

## Day 36

Date:
Passage:

**Today, I am grateful for...**

**Insight verse(s) (write out focus verse for deeper reflection)**

**What this passage reveals about God's character, his purposes, or his ways**

**Adjustments/prayer response: (my response to God's word)**

**Priorities for today**
- 
- 
- 

### A thought for your day...
God can turn your mourning into dancing (Psalm 30:11)

**Reflect back**
What do you sense God has been doing around you, your family, your work, your world? How have you responded?

Daily Spiritual Journal

## Day 37

Date:
Passage:

**Today, I am grateful for...**

**Insight verse(s) (write out focus verse for deeper reflection)**

**What this passage reveals about God's character, his purposes, or his way**

**Adjustments/prayer response: (my response to God's word)**

**Priorities for today**
- 
- 
- 

### A thought for your day...
God will vindicate those who walk in integrity (Psalm 26:1)

**Reflect back**
What do you sense God has been doing around you, your family, your work, your world? How have you responded?

Daily Spiritual Journal

## Day 38

Date:
Passage:

**Today, I am grateful for...**

**Insight verse(s) (write out focus verse for deeper reflection)**

**What this passage reveals about God's character, his purposes, or his ways**

**Adjustments/prayer response: (my response to God's word)**

**Priorities for today**
- 
- 
- 

### A thought for your day...
Your life is a vapor (James 4:14).
Don't waste precious time on that which does not matter.

**Reflect back**
What do you sense God has been doing around you, your family, your work, your world? How have you responded?

Daily Spiritual Journal

## Day 39

Date:
Passage:

**Today, I am grateful for...**

**Insight verse(s) (write out focus verse for deeper reflection)**

**What this passage reveals about God's character, his purposes, or his ways**

**Adjustments/prayer response: (my response to God's word)**

**Priorities for today**
- 
- 
- 

### A thought for your day...
Live and lead in such a way that you experience
the tangible pleasure of God upon you

**Reflect back**
What do you sense God has been doing around you, your family, your work, your world? How have you responded?

Daily Spiritual Journal

## Day 40

Date:
Passage:

**Today, I am grateful for...**

**Insight verse(s) (write out focus verse for deeper reflection)**

**What this passage reveals about God's character, his purposes, or his ways**

**Adjustments/prayer response: (my response to God's word)**

**Priorities for today**

- 
- 
- 

> **A thought for your day...**
> For those watching your life,
> how big would they assume your God is?

**Reflect back**
What do you sense God has been doing around you, your family, your work, your world? How have you responded?

# End of Journal Reflection

So much value can be gained from taking a longer look at your life and your encounters with God. Patterns of his speaking to you, and working within, around, and through you begin to emerge. Take some time before God now to carefully and prayerfully read back through your journal, reflecting on and answering the following questions.

What five characteristics of God, his purposes or ways were most commonly recorded?

1.
2.
3.
4.
5.

As you embrace these truths about God, how will it make a difference for you personally?

What were the five most common adjustments God called upon you to make in response to his word?

1.
2.
3.
4.
5.

What might God be wanting you to do right now? What else?

What were the five most significant ways you noticed God working around you?

1.
2.
3.
4.
5.

When God shows you how he is working around you, that is his invitation for you to join him. In what ways did you join God? Your reflection on these experiences?

What were the five most common emotions that you experienced and/or recorded during this journaling process?

1.
2.
3.
4.
5.

Our emotions often reveal our inner responses, not just to the circumstances, but also to God as well. What might God be wanting you to learn or change as you move forward?

Finally, take some time to prayerfully reflect back on the entirety of this 40-day season of journaling. What has been the most important insight that you gained from this journaling experience?

Commitment Prayer: Express to God any fresh commitments you are making to him.

Finally, ask God whether he would have you to facilitate a group with others to jointly spend 40 days together *Abiding in Christ's Presence*. If so, who might you invite?

**Prayer Requests/Answered Prayers**

**Prayer Requests/Answered Prayers**

**Ways I/we have seen God working**

**What I have learned about God's character, purposes, ways**

**Reasons for gratitude**

# Additional BMI Resources for Deepening Your Effectiveness as a Christian Leader

## Spiritual Leadership Coaching Workshop and Certification Process

Join other leaders in learning twelve essential Spiritual Leadership Coaching Skills in a dynamic and interactive 2 ½ day workshop. This training will equip you to become a more skilled listener, joining God's work in others' lives by asking powerful life-changing questions.

Visit www.blackabycoaching.org/workshop to learn more.

## Blackaby Bible Institute

Take online courses including Experiencing God, Living Out of the Overflow, Unlimiting God, When God Speaks, and The Seasons of God.

Visit www.blackabyinstitute.com to learn more.

## The Richard Blackaby Leadership Podcast

The Richard Blackaby Leadership Podcast helps people take their leadership to the next level through interviews with Christian leaders, book reviews and teaching on spiritual leadership topics.

# The Collision

A resource for equipping Christians to purposefully navigate today's digital and media-driven culture by strengthening their biblical foundation, addressing the difficult questions about their faith, and guiding them to thoughtfully engage with today's pop-culture and secular worldviews.

See www.thecollision.org for more information.

# About the Authors

**Dr. Richard Blackaby** is the president of Blackaby Ministries International (www.blackaby.org). He has authored or co-authored 34 books and speaks internationally on leadership in the church, business, and home. He regularly works with Christian CEOs of major companies in the USA and around the world,  helping them align their life and business with God's agenda. Richard has also served as a pastor and a seminary president. He lives with his wife, Lisa, in Atlanta. They have three children and eight grandchildren.

*Twitter: @richardblackaby*
*Facebook: Dr. Richard Blackaby*
*Blog: www.RichardBlackaby.com*

**Dr. Bob Royall** serves as Director of Coaching for Blackaby Ministries International. The common thread that ties together the many facets of Bob's career as a collegiate minister, seminary professor, pastor, and coach has been his passion for shaping transformational leaders. As Director of Coaching, Bob oversees  all aspects of the Blackaby Ministries International coaching and coach training ministry, while also coaching executives, pastors, and teams. He teaches and speaks on coaching, spiritual formation, leadership, change, and team-building. Bob and his wife, Teresa, live in the Atlanta area. They enjoy outdoor sports and traveling to spend time with their three children and five grandchildren.

*Email: b.royall@blackaby.org*
*LinkedIn: bobroyall*
*Facebook: bobroyall*

www.ingramcontent.com/pod-product-compliance
Lightning Source LLC
Chambersburg PA
CBHW061247040426
42444CB00010B/2289